Tom and Pam

by Kristin Cashore
illustrated by Bob Brugger

Editorial Offices: Glenview, Illinois • Parsippany, New Jersey • New York, New York
Sales Offices: Needham, Massachusetts • Duluth, Georgia • Glenview, Illinois
Coppell, Texas • Sacramento, California • Mesa, Arizona

ISBN: 0-328-13149-0

6 7 8 9 10 V010 14 13 12 11 10 09 08 07

Tom and Tip are on the farm.

They want to see the town.

Tom and Tip are in the town.

Help!

Get us back to the farm!

Pam and Mops are in town.

They want to see the farm.

Pam and Mops are on the farm.

Help!

Get us back to town!

Tom and Tip use a tractor.

Pam and Mops use a cab.

They like where they are.

Read Together

People live in the city, in the country, in deserts, in the mountains, and in the jungle. People live all over the Earth! Some places have many people. Some places do not have many people.

Where do you live? Do many people live there?